Out of Work, Over Fifty:
Copyright © by Tamela Ge
First Edition 2011

ISBN: 978-1-257-55057-9

Written and published by Tamela Georgi
Design & layout by Amy-Lynn Bourne {amy.bourne@telus.net}

* The advice offered in this book must be considered in conjunction with the reader's personal situation and applicable local, regional, national, and international laws.

Dear Reader:

The stuff above is really saying you're not supposed to make copies of this book in whole or in part in any form without the permission of the author.

Here's where I'm supposed to promise huge fines and other dire consequences to the people who dare to do that. Well, unless you make Big Bucks doing that, I'm not going to track you to the ends of the Earth. I'll be too busy writing other books.

I want to keep the cost reasonable--about the price I would pay for a good job search book if I was out of work (and I'm a cheapskate even when I've got a regular job). That's partly so you won't be tempted to make illegal copies. But mostly I want the people who could really use this book to be able to afford it.

By the way, this book is intended as a book of tips, not a comprehensive career planning guide. I hope that the ideas here will help you in your job hunt. I'd love to hear some success stories.

All the best,

Tamela Georgi

Why would you want to buy this book? There's so much good, free information out there and with a click of the mouse, it's yours.

But much of the information you'll find about job search for mature workers is dead serious, clinical, even gloomy.

I didn't need that when I was out of work. I needed something to calm my fears, give me some good practical tips that might actually work and even, at times, make me smile again.

Read on.

About the Author

Gee, I hate writing these things. Here goes:

I started as a career librarian in 1983 while going to journalism school. I got hooked on the whole idea of helping people plan their careers. Since then I have taught job search and career planning workshops to hundreds of people while having the time of my life. I was also chasing down that one elusive publisher who would put my novel(s) in the limelight. It's taken a long time to figure out that I could combine my two passions: Writing and career planning.

You're holding the result. Hope you like it.

And don't even THINK of asking for my picture.

--Tamela Georgi, B. Ed.; Communication Arts Diploma with Print Journalism Major

Acknowledgements

To my Sweetie, your unconditional support over 30 years has made everything outstanding in my life possible.

To Cathie, my writing inspiration.

To Amy, designer extraordinaire.

To my Readers, the smartest people on Earth, I love you.

TABLE OF CONTENTS

Introduction

> *No matter what people say to make you feel better—family, friends, co-workers—it's a heavy blow. You can't help but think if you were faster, smarter, younger, this may not have happened.*
>
> *But it did.*
>
> *How do you deal with it?*

THE GOOD THING about not being 20 anymore is that you've likely weathered a few major life blows. And you're still here to tell about them. This recent downsizing or life circumstance is the same—you will get through this.

For myself, I should have seen it coming. When your office walls are literally torn down to reconfigure the office space and your desk sits upended by the back door, it should be a hint to any logical person that their job might be in jeopardy.

Not me. I didn't even have an updated resume. Denial can blind you to the stark facts: I was going to be laid off, and soon.

But I was a good worker. I hardly took breaks. I used my time well. I treated my clients with the respect and dignity they deserved. My colleagues liked me and even asked my advice. There was nothing wrong with my performance as far as I knew: I hadn't had a performance appraisal since I started the job two years before.

But I was still let go. You can sugar coat it but the fact remained they didn't want to see my face on Monday, or ever again, for that matter.

I'd been laid off a couple of times in my long work history, but the closer you get to retirement, the more insecure you feel about getting back on that horse. The irony was, I was a career counselor. That still didn't prepare me for the avalanche of feelings that came crashing down on my head. There is part of me that will feel the rejection for a long time. But as one friend told me, life rolls on in spite of what happens to you.

Then a funny thing happened. Another employer had been watching my work. I was encouraged to apply for the next opening, and I got it.

It occurred to me that other people my age were facing the same thing. Someone might be interested in advice, not only from a career counselor, but a career counselor who was laid off and over 50. So Out of Work, Over 50 was born.

You might not have been laid off. Maybe you lost your job when you had to move for your spouse's job. Maybe you are in a physically-demanding job and need to find something more sedentary. Whatever your circumstance, here's the good news: You have everything you need to venture in a new direction. You have the talent, the experience, the tough skin that life has given you. But most of all, you have the heart.

This is a little book of tips to get you thinking. The rest is up to you. So for those of us who aren't 20 anymore, keep reading.

Worst Case Scenarios 2

Get the monsters out from under the bed.
What's the worst that could happen? Go ahead, write down your fears. **All of them.** Write fast without thinking.

This exercise is not intended to scare the living crap out of you. It's intended to bring those monsters out of the dark and expose them in plain black and white.

Tackle each fear.

I'll be out of work for a year or more.
No one can predict how long you'll be out of work. Don't read the gloom-and-doom statistics, especially the ones about older workers. That's all they are, statistics. They don't know you. They don't know what you're capable of.

What does my spouse really think? That I could have done something to keep my job? I really need their emotional and financial support right now. I'm afraid they will lose respect for me. They might even leave.
The loss of a job is one of the biggest stresses on a relationship. It will test both of you. Yes, there's a

possibility that it could put big cracks in a relationship that might, ultimately, break it apart. Or it might show that each of you is stronger than you ever thought.

I might have to apply for welfare.

Maybe you will. Government supports are there for a reason. Most of us need help in some form at different times of our lives. Based on your history, you know it will be a temporary situation until you land on your feet again.

Don't discount extended family. You might not be on the best of terms with them or your pride won't let you ask for help. But guess what? That's what families do. You wouldn't refuse to help them if they really needed you, would you? And some day they will.

Sometimes you just have to be the recipient of kindness instead of the giver. Soon it will turn around and you'll be the one helping someone else again. Don't take away their opportunity to help you now.

I'll lose the house.

Okay, maybe you will. Maybe you'll have to rent. Maybe, for a time, you will have to move in with a friend or relative. Again, would you not do the same for them?

What do I tell everyone? I'm not an "x" anymore.

No, you're not. When people ask, briefly say that you are no longer at the Widget Corporation. Then tell them what you are looking for now. Instead of avoiding people because you are dreading having to explain what happened, use them to help you connect with your next job. Your upbeat attitude will make the difference.

I look my age. Who's going to hire a 55-year-old receptionist or (fill in the blank)?

Someone who sees the value of life experience and enthusiasm for the job, that's who. And they'll be lucky to get you.

IF you are worried about your appearance, now is the time to take a good look in the mirror. Do you think you could use a new hairstyle? Different clothes? There are ways to do this even on a restricted budget.

I haven't written a resume in years.

You have it in you to write a great one. In this book you'll find some secrets to powerful resumes.

You are old enough to have had a few hard knocks in your life. Think back. At the time they were rough, maybe more than rough. But a year or two later, did what happen make you look at what was really important? Did it ultimately change you for the better?

This is another of those times. True, you are older now and may feel less confident about bouncing back. But you've bounced back in the past and you will bounce back now.

Take inventory of where you're at now

3

Notes

NOW THAT THE monsters are down on paper, it's time to take a calmer look at where you stand.

Here are some questions to get you thinking. Write down your answers in point form.

- What did you do in your last job?

- How long have you been out of work?

- What job opportunities do you see at the moment?

- What's your money situation?

- Who do you provide for?

- Are there other adults working in your household who can provide income for the family until you find new work?

- Do you have reliable transportation?

- Could you move for a new job? Consider family responsibilities, cost of moving.

- Do you need to upgrade some skills to get a new job in your field?

- How long are you willing to spend on this? A few months? A year? Two years? Could you take courses part time and still work full time?

- Do you see your age as a barrier to employment? In what ways?

- Do you have special circumstances like an injury that would affect your job search?

- Do you feel ready for a job search? Why or why not?

- What other things do you need to consider?

Sample Inventory:

When you've answered these questions, your Inventory will look something like this:

- ☑ Sales rep for a pharmaceutical company

- ☑ Laid off two weeks ago

- ☑ Locally, there are few job opportunities that pay what I was earning on my last job.

- ☑ I have savings that would last for two months of living expenses. After that, I'm dipping into my retirement funds.

- ☑ We have two kids in college and pay about half their expenses—the rest they have earned in part-time jobs and scholarships. One is about to graduate.

☑ Spouse works part-time but could ask for more, possibly up to full-time, hours.

☑ I have a reliable vehicle and could commute to work up to two hours each day.

☑ I can't move to a new job because I need to be available for an elderly parent. Besides, my house wouldn't sell right now, or sell at a loss, since there are lots of houses on the market in my neighborhood and have been for over a year.

☑ However, I'd consider options like renting the basement suite (now that the kids have moved out) for income.

☑ I'd be willing to upgrade my education for up to one year. I'd prefer part-time studies, especially online courses, while I work full-time.

☑ I sometimes struggle to keep up with new technology, especially computer programs at work.

☑ I haven't had to look for a job in seven years. My resume is out of date and I don't know how job interviews have changed. Since I was laid off in a very abrupt way, I feel uncomfortable asking my old supervisor for a job reference. My other references are over seven years old.

☑ Another thing I need to consider is that I'm still in shock over losing that last job. I need to build up my confidence to get ready for a new job search.

Note that circumstances can always change and you'll want to update your Inventory when they do. It's surprising how one change can affect other aspects of your life.

But for now, this is where you're at, your starting point on the road to a new job.

Hopes and Dreams  4

YOUR BIGGEST QUESTION right now is probably: What will my next job be? You're telling yourself to be practical. You're out of work and you can't be fussy. Just get anything for now.

Take a breather.

Whether you've just been laid off or have been looking for work for months: Get alone with yourself. Go for a walk in the park. Take a drive in the country. Walk the dog. Being alone in nature is a great way to clear your head. Take a notebook along to jot down your thoughts.

Let the tension leave your shoulders. Just for a little while.

Think about the things you love to do, the things you would do for free. Take a few notes about what you're thinking about.

Are you nuts? The wolf is at the door. It's not about what I'd like to do, it's about what I have to do!

Your fiercest competition for the good jobs: People who absolutely love what they do.

Think about it. This is an employers' market. Lots of people, yes, with more experience, more talent, more youth, more (fill in the blank) are looking for work, just like you. To the employer, it's like a candy store. So many choices. Do I choose the licorice whips or the hot tamales? They can get someone who is not only qualified, they love what they do.

The person who loves what they do comes to work with a smile on their face, is willing to go the extra mile, and is willing to stay late if necessary. If they are required to go for training, they'll see it as a great opportunity. Wouldn't you rather hire someone like that?

Most of us go about the job hunt backwards. We see a job opening and think of the ways we could bend ourselves into it. Kind of like a pretzel.

It just makes sense to look at yourself first before trying to mold yourself into what you think that employer wants. They aren't that naïve. Most of them can spot a phony.

Instead, start with who you are.

Who are you, anyway? What are your hopes and dreams?

What are you passionate about?

As a career counselor, one of the questions that will tell me more about a person than their job title is, what do you do in your spare time?

What do you think about a lot, talk about a lot? What are you doing when you lose all sense of time?

♦ *Discuss local politics and how things could be improved?*

♦ *Organize the next neighborhood garage sale?*

♦ *Research your family tree?*

♦ *Plan your next trip?*

♦ *Coach basketball?*

♦ *Troll the second-hand bookstores for old science fiction?*

♦ *Plan a kitchen renovation?*

Okay, so likely no one is going to pay you for doing your own home renovations. But think of the skills you are using. Obviously you love to do them, because you've done them in your valuable spare time. Think of the people you are helping, or are helping you, while you do them. That's likely the way you prefer to interact with other Earthlings.

And yeah, maybe there is a job out there that can use some of those skills.

What are your top three favorite skills?

Think of things that few people can do as well as you can. Can you get a diverse team to work well together? Have you never missed a deadline? Did past employers always seek you out to do a certain job?

Don't just think of what you did on past jobs. Think of everything you've done and enjoyed, not just as work experience.

What are your values?

What is important to you? Having time for your family? Making a good income? Giving back to the community? Getting recognition for a job well done?

Make a note of your top three values. They will play a major role in any decision you make about jobs.

When job opportunities come along (and they will), measure them against your strongest values.

Maybe it's family. If you have the chance at a great job but it requires you to be on the road for long hours and away from home, this could be a major conflict. On the other hand, a temporary job out of town with its quick cash injection might be what the family needs right now while you search for something closer and more permanent.

Think about jobs you've had that haven't worked out. They might have been at odds with some of your top values.

But your next job will be in line with those values, because you know what they are and you are now paying attention.

Combine two loves.

I once knew a man who was a dentist and a pilot. He could fly himself to remote communities, hop out of the plane, and walk into the dentist office. There was no need for his company to hire a pilot for him or find a dentist once the pilot was hired.

Do you know how much competition he had for the job? My guess is slim to none. How many people have that unique combination of skills?

That's an extreme case, but we all have a couple of things we're very good at and have a passion for. The two things might not seem to go together at first. It's your job to think about how you might make a living using the combination of these two things (it can be more than two, but let's keep it simple for now).

I have a friend with many talents. She owns two horses and has a passion for all things horsey. She's also a gifted website designer. I asked her why she'd never combined the two.

If you owned a riding stable and wanted to create or update your website, who would you rather hire? Someone who is a whiz at websites and knows nothing equine, or someone who is a whiz at websites AND knows and loves horses?

She approached a horse farm she knew that wanted to sell more of their stock. They asked her to redesign their website. She could even give the photographer advice. The photos of the horses on the website should show them in the best possible light for potential buyers.

The owners were thrilled with the result. Her reputation is now spreading through word-of-mouth recommendations in the tight-knit horse community.

Another friend's two loves are libraries and children. When she began volunteering for a children's reading program at a library, great things began to happen. When people feel your passion for something they often try to make things happen for you. Based on her volunteer experience, two jobs opened up for her (see volunteer section).

Career planning and writing are two of my top loves so I often write about career topics. Also, I've been out of work and over 50. I'd like to help just one other person get through what I went through and come out the other side. The result is the book you're reading.

So what are your two loves? Baseball and helping people? History and writing? Non-profits and managing small teams?

If you can find someone who is looking for your unique combination of skills and interests, your competition for that job will be extremely small.

Where would you like to be in two years?

The answer may surprise you. You might see yourself doing something entrepreneurial. Maybe you see yourself and your family living in a different part of the country. You might be doing a job that is drastically different from what you have done in the past.

What elements of this new life would be essential to your happiness? Paint a picture in your mind of the life you want to have.

Now what steps do you need to take to reach that goal?

Will you need to talk to people in your new field? Will you need more training, more experience? Will you need to volunteer to gain that experience? How much money will you have to save once you get a job?

Do you believe you can do all this? The answer should be 'yes'. Say it out loud. Are you surprised at the strength in your voice?

What are you going to do today to make that life happen?

Your plan should ultimately say what you will do now, today, towards reaching that goal. If you can't spend even 15 minutes on it today, then it ain't gonna happen. Two years will fly by on gossamer wings.

The decisions you make today will affect the life you'll have in two years. Your present job search should make sense to that goal.

The Job Hunt

START WITH YOUR Ideal Job Targets.
These would combine one or more of your passions and at least two of your best skills. There will be fewer people who can compete with you for these jobs. Think of three Ideal Job Targets.

Secondary Job Targets
These might involve a slightly lesser passion for you, or only one skill of your top three. They might be jobs you've held in the past and wouldn't mind doing again.

When choosing these secondary targets, think not only of what you are getting out of it (a salary, a chance to learn new skills, etc.) but what you have to offer the employer.

Okay-For-Now Job Targets
These are jobs where you still have something valuable to contribute. You also can learn things that will be useful in your future.

Keep in mind that your toughest competition for these jobs will be the people who rate them Number One. And ask yourself, given your experience, would it be a real stretch to convince the employer that you want this job? If it's hard for you to make that connection, it's going to be almost impossible for the employer to buy it.

Research all your job targets.

Find out all you can about your job targets. Get on the Net and start searching for information on them, starting with your Ideal Job Targets.

Most jobs are about solving some kind of problem for someone. What problems can you solve? What unique talents or experience can you bring to this job?

Would you have to move to do this job? Does it pay what you thought it would? Would you have to have more education, or could you train on the job?

Is there a similar job that would be more acceptable to you? Do you need to change one or more of your targets?

What's happening in the industry now? Has the economy affected it or not? What's happening locally?

Before you start talking to people in this field, you'll want to do all the research you can.

You may have contacts in this area without knowing it. That's why it's good to talk to friends and family about it. They might have a co-worker whose spouse once worked at that company. You never know where your contacts will lead you.

The reality is, it's your contact with other Earthlings that will get you a job.

I've mentioned spouses and partners of people you know. Over the years it's surprising how many job contacts my clients have found through them. Think about your friends and acquaintances. Do you know what their partners do? If you have a significant other yourself, do you know all of their friends and acquaintances and their corresponding partners? Bet you don't. And bet you that one of them has some valuable inside information on a job for you.

Think back to jobs you've held. How many times did you learn of a job opening in your company before the boss ever did? It might have been a work friend who told you that she was going to quit because she was moving to the other side of the country. It happens all the time. And you were sitting on this information that could have been priceless to someone looking for work, someone who would be ideal for the job. In fact, you may have passed this information on to another friend who ended up getting the job.

That's why it's important to let people know that you're looking for a job. It's not enough to tell people that you're looking for work. Be specific. The human brain can work with specific. Tell them your top two Ideal Job Targets to start.

Their immediate response might be, 'Sorry. I haven't heard about any jobs like that'. But once that seed is planted in their mind, the memory will come back when they hear of an appropriate job opening. And they will call you.

Keep an open mind when it comes to job openings.

You've likely had a job in the past that didn't sound too spiffy when you read the description but turned out to be one of the best jobs of your career.

For example, maybe you have a love for fundraising. Ideally, you would be involved with fundraising for a sports team. There's a job advertised — fundraising, yes, but for a charity you're not familiar with.

Do your research on that organization. They could use your fundraising skills and you could use the experience. Would you be willing to stay with the job for a decent period of time?

Then, in a year or two, if an opportunity to work in fundraising for a soccer team comes open, you might decide to apply for it. Or you might like the organization you've been working for so much that you decide to stay. Either way, you've honed those fundraising skills and you have become a valuable employee doing something you love.

Sometimes you can bend the rules.

Once I came home from a long trip to see a great job advertised. Rats! It was a couple of days past the deadline.

When I called to explain the situation — that I was away and only now read the ad — the secretary said that it was too late. People were being interviewed as we spoke.

I had nothing to lose at that point. I said that was too bad since I had direct experience counseling injured workers to find jobs and gave her some details. It was exactly what they were looking for and I knew it.

There was a pause on the other end. She quickly put me through to a supervisor, and from there I got an interview, and then the job.

I could have given up when I read that the deadline was past. I could have given up after I called and found out that people were already being interviewed.

If there's something about a job that intrigues you but you don't think you can apply for it (for whatever reason), take a chance and try anyway. You never know what opportunity might sail your way.

Make some (gulp) cold calls.

Call potential employers and ask about job openings.

Respect their time. Ask them if they have a few minutes to talk to you and don't be pushy. Read the hints that your time is over.

Don't use one of those complicated 'telephone conversation' graphs where you have to follow the arrows if the person says 'no', etc., unless you are one of the five people on the planet who can follow such things.

Instead, plan on what you want to say. You can jot down a couple of key words that will remind you of the points you want to make. Your whole 'speech' should be very short:

You are looking for job opportunities in this industry. This is your experience in this industry. Add one or two of your top achievements, matched to what would be of particular interest to them. Then let the person ask you questions.

If they don't know of any job openings, either now or in the near future, you can ask if they've heard of openings in other places. Some people don't like to ask this, thinking that an employer might be insulted by talking about their competition. But it has produced job leads.

As much as possible, let them talk. Ask questions that require more than yes or no for an answer. You never know what might come up. They might even like what you are saying so much that they ask you to come in to talk to them. At this point they want to size you up, to see if the confident voice matches the person, or maybe just be able to put a face to your name.

By the way, it sounds crazy, but talk with a smile on your face. No, they can't see it over the phone but they can 'hear' it.

If there is an opening advertised, this makes the cold call that much easier. You are calling to get details of the position. You might also find out some details that are not in the advertisement, giving you an advantage. I usually ask, 'What else are you looking for in a person for this position?'.

The good thing about talking to an employer is that if there is an opening, you can mention on your cover letter that you spoke to him and from your conversation you felt even more motivated to apply for this job. You can also tailor your resume to match your achievements to the needs he spoke about.

Getting a resume out of the blue from a Boomer with more experience than a CEO can be a little intimidating. If you talk to the employer before you send a resume, not only can you gain valuable inside information to tailor your resume to that job, you can also make a great first impression. You are no longer a stranger.

Don't let a terror of cold calls keep you paralyzed on the coach with Fido and a cup of hot cocoa. If cold calls are the scariest thing about your job hunt, get them done early. It sets the pace for the rest of the day. Yes, there will be one or two people who don't have the time to talk, are perhaps abrupt or even rude. (That might tell you that you wouldn't want to work for them). But overall it's a small percent. Even if the calls don't always go as you planned, you did it! By four o'clock you'll feel that you have accomplished something significant.

Can't get past reception?

Try calling the office a half hour before they open or a half hour after they close. Bosses often come in early and stay late and sometimes they are the ones answering the phones at these times.

Why doesn't anyone call me back?

You've dropped off resumes, dozens of them, and not one employer has called you back.

First of all, don't assume that the right person even got your resume. When you drop one off, be sure to call back in a day or so to connect with the person with the power to hire you, to see if he got your resume.

As a career counselor I'm shocked to learn how many people don't make this little phone call that could make the difference between getting an interview or not. A client of mine called back and eventually the employer admitted that she was being seriously considered for an interview, then they lost her resume! She quickly provided another one, got the interview, and landed the job.

Don't be shy about following up on this. 'Hello, Ms. White. I'm very interested in working for your firm and I delivered my resume a couple of days ago. I'm just calling to confirm that you received it and see if you've had a chance to look at it.'

If they have a few minutes to talk, you can add a couple of points about why you would love to have this job. Keep it short, and take their lead. They may ask you questions like a mini interview.

Your new employer might not be as far away as you might think.

Chances are, someone outside your company noticed your work, saw that you were laid off, and might be interested in hiring you as you read this paragraph.

Think of all the contacts you've made with that old company, and not just the obvious ones. Who were you in contact with in the course of a day? Everyone from the courier company to organizations you called occasionally. You developed some kind of relationship with each of them.

They might be hiring right now and the best part is—you're not a stranger to them. It could be enough to get your foot in the door for an interview.

If you need a job NOW!

Say you have to get 'any' job for now. You still have some choices. Maybe there are just a few job openings in your town. One is at a donut shop. One is as a clerk in a home supply store. Another is pumping gas.

Which would you choose?

That depends on your passions and goals. Even though it might seem a long way from today to your ideal situation, you can look at one of these jobs as an opportunity. Maybe you want to own your own small bakery one day. The donut shop job can give you an insight into customers—what they buy, what they don't, what they wished the shop sold, their favorite time to come in, the things they say about the place. This could be valuable research to a person who wants to own their own business one day.

Even when you have to make fast choices, think about how this job can somehow enhance your future plans. You'll be a much happier employee.

Pretend you don't have unemployment insurance.

A word about unemployment insurance: It can be a huge relief to know you have it. But human nature being what it is we tend not to start a serious job hunt until we're reaching the end of our unemployment insurance. At that time a note of desperation creeps in.

What's also dangerous about leaving things to the last minute is you aren't used to a schedule. Maybe you've made it a habit of staying up a little later each night and sleeping in a little more each day. And why not? You don't have to get up to go to a job, right?

Wrong. When you're out of work, looking for work is your new job. It can be the toughest job you'll ever do.

So pretend you don't have the safety net. Take your job search seriously — now. You don't know what kind of opportunities you might miss by waiting for the final bell.

One of the worst things about losing a job is losing the structure in your life. You wake up each morning and everyone's got somewhere to go except you. When the spouse and kids leave the house in the morning, you're left alone to study the walls.

It can feel like a punishment. Forget the odd days when you were at work and wishing you could be (on the golf course, in the pool, fill in the blank). Now you have all the time in the world and all you want to do is to get back to work.

Not only are you 'freed' from work, you were let go from the structure. And we human beings need structure. We need to feel that we've done something productive today.

Make a schedule. You will get out of bed early. You will do things. You will follow a plan.

Ideally, if you want to get a new job, you should be spending at least six hours a day on it. That doesn't mean you have to spend six hours sweating over a resume, although there could be days like that. No, six hours could include putting together that interview outfit (or the talk-to-prospective-boss outfit), running to the store for paper to print out resumes, calling friends and acquaintances you know to see if they've heard of job openings, etc.

Decide how much time you will spend each day on your job search and stick to it. You say that there just aren't enough jobs you can apply for in your town? Then research your options. Would your unemployment insurance cover (or at least allow you take) a course on setting up your own business? There's much more to a job hunt than just flooding the market with resumes.

What can you do today that would make the most impact on your job search?
Start with that task.

Is it cold calls? Okay. Try one first thing in the morning. It might be tough, but once you've done it you'll pat yourself on the back. After it's done, the other tasks will seem easy compared to the one you were dreading. By five o'clock you'll feel like you've accomplished something that day. Then relax. Remember that your job right now is looking for a job, and today you did good.

What is one thing you could do today that will change your life for the better?

If looking for work is your job right now, it's important but it shouldn't take over your life.

Other people work five days a week and then give themselves the weekend off. You've worked at least as hard as they do trying to find a job and you deserve your guilt-free weekend.

Besides your job hunt, what else are you doing to improve your life? Maybe it's a daily walking routine to improve your fitness, maybe it's a plan to get more sleep. Or maybe it's planning a date night with your significant other. Doesn't have to be expensive. Homemade pizza by candlelight, every Tuesday night. You might just start a tradition.

References  6

YOU SHOULD HAVE three to five good references before you start a serious job search.

Ideally some of your best references would be from your last job. But if you were laid off, there might be uncomfortable feelings about asking someone at your old company for a reference.

Help! I can't use my last boss as a reference.

You can go back to your previous job, although that might be several years old and your references there may have moved on. That's why it's good to keep in contact with your references. Great references can be used several years after you've left a job, as long as you've stayed current with them.

Okay, hindsight is 20-20. You need references now.

Think about everyone you were in contact with at your old company. If you can't use your former supervisor for a reference (and many of us can't), think about someone else in the company who has seen your work and can vouch for your performance.

It might be a supervisor from another department. They might have seen what was coming and felt bad for you, because you were a hard worker, conscientious, and they didn't agree with the decision to let you go. This person could be a good reference for you now. They might even take a little defiant pride in their role to help you get a new job.

Maybe you had a supervisor who left the company at the same time you did. Call them up and ask if they would be a reference for you. You never know, they might also have a job lead.

Can't think of anyone in your old company? How about a company you did regular business with? Maybe someone who contracted with your company to do some service. It doesn't hurt to ask.

I got fired. No reference for me.

Number One, be sure that the new jobs you apply for don't put you in the same situation as the old one.

For example, you were fired because they thought you were an incompetent manager. If that was your first shot at management, you might want to stay away from it in your next job.

Obviously you can't use your old boss, the one who fired you, for a reference for new jobs. However, the same thing from above applies. People have been known to use supervisors in other departments who may be able to comment on the person's work performance, work ethics, etc. You'd be surprised how often this happens.

Some people cultivate these references when it looks like they might be let go. A supervisor equal in power to your own boss is often not afraid of being a good reference for you. This type of reference is valuable, especially if you've been with the one organization for several years.

You also might want to consider a reference from an outside company who knew your work.

Be aware that a potential employer may see through this and guess that you had some trouble with your former supervisor. They may ask you about it. Be prepared to explain the situation as diplomatically as possible. Role play your answer with a friend who can play the part of a cynical interviewer.

Volunteer your way to a great reference.

Another way to gain references is to volunteer. If you've been volunteering while you were still working then you likely have at least one reference who can vouch for your work ethic.

It's not too late. You can get great references from volunteering now.

Give your reference a heads-up.

Let them know what job you are applying for. A quick email is all it takes. You can say that a Ms. Jacobs may be calling for a reference on a widget sales job and she will be especially interested in your last year's sales performance and your ability to work well in a large team.

That's all you need to do. You aren't giving your reference a script, but you are giving them an idea of what's important to the employer.

Some people like to coach their references on exactly what to say. I prefer to let them find their own words.

The Secret Weapon Resume

CREATING A GREAT resume is work. It can take a whole day. The good news is, once you have something that you are proud of, it's fairly easy to make changes when you apply for a different job.

There's so much information out there and a lot of it is conflicting. Who is THE expert on resumes?

The real expert on resumes is that potential employer you want to attract. You can't get inside his mind but with some detective work you can figure out the ideal candidate he's looking for. And that will take you a few steps closer to the prize.

Do I hire a resume writer?

Short answer: No. You have to put the work into something if you want it to be good. And no matter how good that writer is, they usually don't know you very well. And don't even think about getting your cousin Sue to do one because she says she's great at it. Your resume will probably look a lot like cousin Sue's.

People who aren't writers feel that 'real' writers have some kind of magic when it comes to resumes. But the truth is

I've seen some fantastic resumes come from people who have no writing background at all. And some of the best writing I've ever read came from an adult literacy student who lived in the far North. You have it in you to write your own terrific resume, one that will stand out from the crowd.

How do I start?

What four or five essential things would a person in this position have to have? The job description should list these things, but sometimes it's not in any priority. Figure out the top four or five. Then think of all your skills, experience, education, etc. that match. This will become the heart of your resume.

If you're really struggling to match your abilities to those top four, you should probably look at another job. If you are having trouble seeing yourself doing that job, then that goes double for the employer.

Whenever possible, create a different resume for each job you apply for, focused on that employer.

Remember the good old days when you sent out your resume to twenty or more employers? When times were good and jobs were plentiful, you'd get several call backs.

Isn't working so well now, is it? When there are many people competing for the same jobs, employers can be picky. They can wait until the ideal person comes along.

You need to tailor your resume to that job and that employer. Sounds like a lot of work, and it can be.

Some people like to have an information file of all their experience. From there, they pick and choose what's relevant for each job opening and build a resume.

If you are applying for similar jobs, you might only need to make a few changes. But you have to match your skills and abilities to each job.

Employers want to know that you have done your research on their company and the job being offered. You have to show them how your skills and experience fit. It's up to you to connect the dots for them.

Also, if you have experience in more than one field, you may need a different resume for each. That doesn't mean you can't use some of the experience you got from one to another, if it's relevant.

There's the key word: Relevant. The employer wants to know your experience that is RELEVANT to the job opening.

You might have two or three 'base' resumes, and from there you will change each somewhat to match your skills to the job.

For example, I have a writing resume that I use when applying for writing contracts—that particular employer wants to see what I've written that's relevant to the project I'm applying for. Then there's my history resume that I use when applying for archives work. Then there's my career counselor resume.

You might have one resume that targets your ability to train employees if you are applying for a job as a trainer. In that case you could use your experience in training in several different fields, not just the one you're applying for.

For example, if you've trained people while working in museums and again in factories, it might seem like the two don't have much in common. But they do. A good teacher is a good teacher, no matter what the subject.

After you've put in the work and sweat into your resume draft and feel that it's very good, then by all means have someone look it over for typos, grammar, etc. But don't let them change the essence of it. I ask people, "Does this resume feel like you? Sound like you? Can you hand it to an employer feeling confident about it?"

When you write your own resume you will use words and terms you normally use, not super resume words that an outsider thinks look cool. In an interview, employers will often ask you random questions by looking at your resume. "I see you liaised with city officials on waste management". Your answer shouldn't be, "Huh?" When you write your own resume, you understand what's in it. You'll remember what's in it.

What goes on a cover letter, and what goes on a resume?

Think of the cover letter as a friendly introduction. It's where you say you are very interested in this job and you generate some excitement in the heart of the employer that—hey, this could be the person I'm looking for.

It's where you can summarize some key points of your resume. You can also use it to remind the employer that you spoke on the phone, or met at a conference, etc.

The resume gets down to the brass tacks. It's where you show the employer in detail how your experience matches what they want.

Write the resume first, then the cover letter.

How many seconds?

Take a double-spaced typed page and start reading. Stop when you get halfway down the page. That's the length of time some employers take to skim your resume. You've got only seconds to make an impression.

I once had a trades employer admit that he read resumes while driving down the highway in his truck. If a resume didn't attract his attention right away, it got thrown into the back seat and he grabbed the next one.

To some extent, mimic their wording.

I've had employers tell me, "I don't know what it was about your cover letter and resume, but they were dead-on."

That was because I took some of the wording from the actual ad or job posting and used that wording in my cover letter and resume.

You don't want to go through the whole posting and just copy their phrases, but do use two or three of their key words.

What about an Objective?

This is optional, and if you use one it's best to keep it short and sweet. Too many objectives meander like a never-ending river of words. Too often, an Objective sounds self important and phony. Some sound like they're after the boss's job. Don't give them a chance to weed you out on the first line of your resume. Better to use this information in your cover letter, where you can word it in a friendly way.

List achievements, not just job duties.

I once was sent to help counsel a large factory of people who were being laid off. There were about 300 employees with the same job description, the same job duties.

Can you imagine what would happen if all 300 listed their job duties and nothing else under their work experience? You'd have, on paper, 300 people with identical experience. The only difference would be the number of years each had put in. No, just listing your job duties won't cut it. How would that make you stand out from the other 299 people now applying for jobs in that market?

You can still put your key duties in, but blend them with your achievements in that area.

What are achievements?

Employers like to know that you have been a valuable employee in your previous jobs. If past behavior is a good indication of future behavior, your achievements are very important.

In fact, this could be the most important part of your job search. It is probably the most important tip in this book. More than anything else, it is your best achievement matched to the employer's needs that will get you noticed.

So spend a good chunk of time thinking about your achievements on each of your past jobs.

What made you special on that job?

Exactly how were you valuable? Did you save time or money for your employer? Did you develop a faster, more efficient way of doing something?

Did repeat customers ask for you specifically?

Did you train new employees? This might have been an informal arrangement and not in your job description, but if you did it, put it in your resume. One or more of your references should be able to confirm it.

Were you known as the go-to person when the computer had a hissy fit?

What things do you do that are exceptional, that few people could outdo?

Maybe you want to show that you are punctual. Instead of just saying 'punctual' on your resume, prove it:

--Not late for work in five years

Or--

--Outstanding Attendance Award given for five years running

Awards are great. There are other ways of saying your work stood out:

- The XYZ Newsletter was used as a model for future career publications

- Invited by corporate office to design changes to the forward production line

Employers like numbers. Whenever possible, be able to measure your success:

- Managed large caseload of injured workers with 98 per cent success rate

- Department production increased 30 per cent in the first six months

- Widget sales doubled in the first year

- Scanned and described thousands of photos of the XYZ Collection

The following one lists regular job duties but it was still quite an achievement to juggle all these balls in the air:

- Liaised with Home Care, doctors, various hospital departments, outside agencies, and family to ensure a smooth transition for patient

Maybe your achievement lies in how you did the job:

- Interviewed people from diverse educational and ethnic backgrounds with sensitivity and fairness

Your references or a performance appraisal should be able to confirm your achievements. I've even quoted a sentence from a performance appraisal on my resume:

- Supervisor's performance appraisal stated: 'Kept a level head, even under tight deadlines, heavy workloads and high stress'

I don't like to brag.

Bragging is an empty boast. When you list your achievements, you can back them up either with performance appraisals, awards, or the glowing words from your references. You are presenting yourself in the best possible light, but you aren't bragging. The other 199 people applying for the job aren't worried about tooting their own horns. Neither should you, if you want the job.

Should I 'dumb down' my resume?

You want a job. Like you, there are lots of people out of work, people with lots of experience, who are applying for entry-level jobs. You may even be more qualified than the supervisor or the owner. So you're thinking about hiding some of your qualifications.

The employer's fear: You will take this job and stay only until a better opportunity comes along. Or you will be too bossy. Or you won't listen to direction from your supervisors — probably younger supervisors.

Your resume may be flashing this like a huge neon sign.

Ask yourself: Is that right? Would you take the job, go through their training, and then dump them as soon as the economy picks up a little?

Or is this a field you love, and yes, you've been laid off and need work. But your reputation in this industry is important and you promise to make a commitment on this job and will do the very best job you can. You have never been in the habit of leaving an employer in the lurch.

This employer is offering you a job when jobs are tough to find. He deserves a little loyalty.

The best way to deal with this question is to make contact with the employer. Start by asking about the position. Then, diplomatically, tell them what you've been thinking. That you see this as a wonderful opportunity and you have much to contribute. You would be willing to commit to this position for (a year, two years?) because you believe in the company and--

If you can't make contact with the employer before the competition ends, then your cover letter and resume will have to do the talking for you.

But will they still consider you?

They might if they can see your passion.

My experience shows how old I am.

You can't lie on a resume, but you don't have to list every job you've held since the seventh grade. For example, instead of listing all your work experience, list what you deem relevant for this particular job and use the heading Relevant Experience. This implies that you've left out jobs that you believe are not important to the job you're applying for.

As a general rule, go back no more than ten years of your work experience. There are exceptions. For example, if you are applying for a museum job and fifteen years ago you were on an archeological dig, then by all means put it down. The museum will be very interested to know about the dig and it might be the one thing that makes your resume stand out and get you invited for an interview.

You can also hide the dates of employment a little, even putting them in smaller print, so they don't stand out as much.

Example:

Auctioneer
Big T Auction Mart, Timbuktu (2000 to 2007)

Beware of hidden age giveaways.
You want your resume to get you that interview. Once you've passed to the interview stage there is more of an investment in you. They have taken the time to shortlist and you are one of the chosen. Your chances have shot way up from your time in the resume pile.

Yes, they can now see that you're not 20 anymore and some employers (although they'd never admit it) are reluctant to hire you on the basis of your age. But you're prepared for the interview and can tell them how great you'd be as their new employee.

If you suspect you're not getting interviews because your resume reveals your approximate age, there are a few things you can do:

If you use a Summary, or Highlights of Qualifications at the top of your resume, you don't want to say something like, 'Thirty years' experience in the textile industry', unless you want to advertise your age with another neon sign.

Stating the year of your high school graduation is another age revealer. Don't list the year. If you have a college diploma or degree, then you normally wouldn't put your high school education on your resume. It's assumed that you graduated from high school if you are a college graduate. If you think your college years still date you, you could leave the dates off. You can give that information at an interview.

Yes, there is the chance that you will be eliminated for not providing the years of your education. You have to weigh this against being eliminated because they mistakenly think you're too old for the job.

I've been in one job for ten years.

You probably had a number of jobs for that one employer in that time. So under your experience at Lance Corporation, you will list each job position, starting with your most recent, and write your achievements for each. You are, in essence, treating your experience with that one company as several different jobs.

Unusual interests and experience

When all things (applicants) are equal, how does an employer choose the lucky few who will be interviewed?

Have you ever watched the news on TV at the end of a long day? How much do you remember about the weather forecast, the financial news, the daily antics of politicians? Then a human interest story comes on the air. Maybe it's about a man who builds a flying armchair. Which will you remember?

The human mind remembers the unusual. We're programmed to play the game of 'one of these things is not like the others'.

Besides your achievements and skills relevant to the job you're applying for, your resume can stand out from the pile by adding a couple of things that will stay in an employer's mind long after he reads it. It might be your overseas experience, your dedication to helping the local food bank reach their goal of raising $50,000 in one weekend.

Who have you helped in the past? What do you have a passion for, outside of work?

We're talking unusual and interesting, not what might be considered weird. That's not the kind of employee most people want to deal with. But an interesting person, that's another story. We all want to hear about something exciting and new. It could be the thing that gets your foot in the door of an interview. And once you're there, you can tell them how your achievements make you the ideal candidate.

You can use the Interests category on your resume (not the old category of Hobbies, which implies that you didn't take those activities seriously), and you don't have to put dates to them. Interests show that you are a real person, not just one of the faceless dozens who might be applying for the job.

Highlights of Qualifications

This is optional but I almost always use this section. It's the first thing on my resume but the last thing I write.

That's because it's much easier to write after I've written everything else and can now summarize what's important. I choose three to four key things. These things match my top qualifications to the top qualifications I believe the employer is looking for. I put these items in point form in this section.

Example:

<u>Highlights of Qualifications</u>

- Flexible writer able to handle multiple projects and deadlines

- Solid foundation in career planning from managing specialized career libraries to leading workshops and writing course content

- Experienced researcher: Extensive research and interviews completed for three non-fiction books

The employer for the above position wanted a writer and researcher with a career planning background. I decided that they would be most interested in these three key points of my experience. If education seemed to be very important to that employer, I would have listed it in the

Highlights. Yes, it will also be in the Education section which is usually at the bottom of the resume.

Note that I haven't mentioned the number of years of experience in this Highlights section.

You can also get a little creative to make your resume stand out:

- Lifelong baker, constantly experimenting with recipes

- Lifelong love of history from a college archeological dig to present writing

A note about points and bullets: A list of four to five is the maximum you would want to have in any section. After that, the human eye glazes over and the point of the points becomes moot. They don't stand out anymore.

Now choose a format you really like.

There are hundreds of resume books out there and many more free samples on the Net. You can shop around for the format you like—that's the way it's typed. You already know that your content is fine.

My own resumes go in this order. Feel free to disagree:

1. *Name in bold, at least 16 point font.*

2. *Highlights of Qualifications*

3. *Relevant Experience (heavy on the achievements for each workplace)*

4. *Interests*

5. *Education / Training*

I don't put my references on the resume unless the employer asks for them to be submitted at the same time as the application. More and more employers check references, and what is relatively new, they check them before you even walk through the door. The more traditional way is to ask for references at the job interview where you will hand them a separate sheet with your references.

A few things to think about when typing your resume:

Templates can be fussy. I once spent half an hour trying to convince one that I didn't want a line and a half spacing in one section. They don't listen well.

Unless you're a keyboarding fool, go for simple. Start with a simple Word document. If you use a lot of tabbing and fancy boxes, ask yourself how easy it will be to make changes later. And how well do those fancy details email?

You're aiming for a resume that looks professional and is easy to read.

End — Are you happy with it?

You know that you have the right resume if, when you email it or hand it to an employer, you aren't thinking about your resume. You aren't still questioning your wording under that second job, or wondering if the font is a little over the top. You are confident in what it says and how it looks.

It's ready.

Cover Letters  8

THE BEST COVER letter is a friendly introduction to your resume. Not meatloaf.

Many cover letters that come over the transom for a job opening are, frankly, boring. Kind of like meatloaf and mashed potatoes. If you put a little zest in yours, plus explain how your experience and abilities uniquely match the job, your letter should get noticed. You want to convey your enthusiasm for this job while giving them a reason to take interest in you.

You don't have to be a Hemingway. Write as though you were calling an employer about a job. You want to come across as friendly, professional, competent, respectful. Use your normal flow of speaking.

A cover letter can be your way to connect yourself directly to the job. A resume can't always do that. For example, if you've worked on mutual projects, had mutual clients, or some other connection to that workplace and/or the job, now's your time to say it.

The resume is a more formal document. You can't address anyone directly, and a resume normally does not use the word 'I'.

The cover letter is a little like a conversation on paper.

Imagine that the boss is sitting across from you and you want to tell her, in about one minute, why she should call you for an interview. Your cover letter is like that conversation, on paper.

A cover letter and resume are partners, and, if done well, should get you interviews. That's their job. If you aren't getting interviews, there might be something wrong with one or both of them. If you're getting lots of interviews but no job offers, then your interview skills and presentation might need work.

Make your cover letter stand out.

It's up to you to find those jobs that would be a great match for you. And then you have to convince that employer that you are a great match for their job.

Your cover letter will stand out when the recipient recognizes that you may be the one they're looking for. Not only do you have the qualifications they're asking for, you have extras.

Yes, you're a mature worker and you might be worried about how an employer feels about hiring mature workers. But it's strange how things like that don't seem to matter as much when you are a great match to the job and enthusiastic to boot.

The seed of a great cover letter (and resume) starts with your research. You have to do your homework.

Again, think of yourself like a detective hunting down clues. There's far more to a job than the few lines in an advertisement. Advertising is expensive. Few companies can tell you everything they want in a person for this position in a small advertised block, or even on online postings.

If you can reach the employer and talk about the position, it is a great opportunity to make a connection. They could be starting to make a decision about you over the phone. When you tell them your name they might very well look for your resume when it comes in. If you've made a good impression, then you have just set yourself above a big chunk of your competition.

Do you really want this job? Then you'll put in the time to search the company's website, to call and talk to the boss about what they're looking for, to talk to people you know who might have had business with this company, or someone who used to do the same kind of job.

You want to get beyond the obvious. So do your homework. It will show.

The best time to write a cover letter is after you're finished your resume.

Gather all the information you know about this job. Think about the four essential things needed to do the job and how your experience matches them.

How to write the Cover Letter:

First paragraph:

The first paragraph tells them what job opening you are applying for, but it shouldn't sound stilted:

Which sounds better:

Please accept my application for the job of. . .

Or

I was excited to hear about the opening for the x position. Please accept my resume….

Here's an actual opening paragraph that landed an interview:

I would like to apply for the X position. I am excited about the opportunity to continue to help people in our community find jobs and relevant training on their career paths.

If you've spoken to the boss about the position, you can also mention that in the first paragraph.

Our phone conversation of Jan. 18 encouraged me to apply for this position.

Second paragraph:

The second paragraph should say why you would be ideal for this job. Here's where you go back to what you believe are the top four qualities a person in this position should have. Choose about two for this second paragraph.

In this case, I believed the person for this position would need a strong background in career planning and have experience with a variety of clients:

My passion for helping people with career planning hasn't dimmed since I read my first copy of What Color Is Your Parachute I've been a workshop developer, facilitator, and a career librarian for several career centers in my region. My clients have had a variety of barriers to employment including being: mature workers, injured workers, immigrants, youth, and visible minorities. Together we created effective career plans.

Note that of all the clients I have worked with, I chose to list the kind of clients I would be working with on this new job—again, everything should be relevant to that job opening.

You want to come across as confident but not arrogant. The last sentence recognizes that I didn't do all this on my own—the client was a working partner.

If you've found a job opening that reflects your top two passions, then your second paragraph should jump right in and say so:

I was delighted to discover that you are looking for a writer to design workshops for mature workers. . .

Then you would explain your experience both as a writer and someone who has worked with mature workers.

Third paragraph:

The third paragraph could talk about the third and perhaps fourth most important qualities for a person in this position.

For example, maybe from your research you discovered that this employer had trouble with employees getting along and may even had to let someone go. So one of their priorities is to hire someone who will get along on their team. Have you worked with mutual clients? Worked with the staff on other projects?

I enjoyed working with your staff on the Gerling project last year. I think they would tell you that we developed a good working relationship.

This encourages the employer to ask their staff—Is this true? Did you get along with her? What was she like to work with?

That's a long shot—having direct experience with their staff. If you've never worked on mutual projects you can say how you did work on similar projects with other companies. You want to describe experience that is as close to theirs as possible.

Possible fourth paragraph:

This paragraph can address more of the top four important qualities. In this case the job description also listed these skills:

You also require someone who can read, write, speak, and communicate effectively. I also have a background in journalism and have been trained to gather information and write articles.

Last paragraph:

Many people just thank the employer for their time and consideration at this point. You can also add details to continue to link you to the job, right to the end.

I would love to be invited for an interview. I think you would find me a dedicated worker who shows up on time and has an excellent attendance record. I take pride in my work. I'm looking forward to hearing from you.

After writing this, I wondered if it sounded too personal. But strangely enough, this last paragraph struck a strong cord with that employer. During the interview she revealed that her existing team had attendance problems. It seemed to me that she was looking for a mature person who could be a good influence on her younger staff—not another supervisor who had to constantly remind them to show up on time, but a co-worker who led by example.

How long should it be?

In general, you'll want to keep the cover letter to one page, but there are exceptions. Over the years it's been rare that I've had to go to two pages.

If you are writing two pages, keep editing to see if you can make it one. Maybe some of your information would be better for your resume.

Keep in mind the purpose of both the cover letter and resume. It's to get your foot in the door to that interview. You can discuss details then.

Interview Preparation

9

Congratulations! You've got an interview! Now what?

What problem do they have to solve?

That is, in a nutshell, why employers hire people. They have a problem they want solved. What is their problem?

Ideally, they believe the person they hire, above the others who were short-listed, will help solve this problem.

So, figure out what their problem is and how you as their employee would help solve it.

Think fast: What four things would be ideal for this candidate to have?

The same rule you used to write your resume applies to preparing for the interview. If you were the employer, what top four qualities would you want in this person? It could be a combination of personal qualities, education, past job skills.

It helps if you've done this job before. For practice, think of your last job. What would have been four ideal things for that person to have?

Then before you leave that interview, you want to let them know that you have those things. That doesn't mean that you count them off on your fingers. But you can strongly weave them into your answers to their questions.

Whenever they give you a chance to talk about yourself, think of these four crucial things. Usually at the end of the interview you will have a chance to add some comments as well.

Obviously, if these are four things you believe to be essential to that job, and you have serious doubts that you could do two of them, then reconsider that job.

Do YOU believe you're the best person for this job?

When you look at the job requirements and your own skills, both personal and on-the-job, your experience, your enthusiasm, and the problem that needs solving, you should feel confident that you would do a very good job for this employer.

Why should we hire you?

Really, between you and me, why DO you believe you're the best person for this job? You might reply that another candidate might be younger and have more recent credentials, but there's no way they can match you in experience. Have they helped a company go through a merger? Have they ever had to handle an angry team of managers? (Go ahead, fill in the blank with your own experience).

Comparing resumes, people can seem to be equal. But we know they're not. And one of the great things about interviews is that they can get a chance to see the real you.

Picture your competition.

Guess who your competition is. Make up a really tough competitor. Make a list of their skills and experience. Create this person on paper.

You might think up a younger person with a lot of energy and maybe better, more recent education. Think of what you have to offer and why an employer might choose you instead. For example, Baby Boomers have a reputation for a strong work ethic. When they have to call in sick, they really are. Younger people have often been unfairly called unreliable, taking too much sick time and vacations. This could be your cue to say that you only missed one day due to sickness last year.

Another competitor might be someone your own age but with better management skills. What will you offer the employer to counteract that?

It never ceases to amaze me that the three people I've created in my head are often sitting right there in reception waiting, like me, for their interview.

Much of life is about attitude. If you absolutely believe you are the best person for this job, then that will come across strong and clear. If you don't believe it, then that will come across just as clear.

Past behavior is a predictor of future behavior.

Can people change? Absolutely. An employee who was once constantly late can make a concentrated effort to show up on time. But history does tend to repeat itself.

Like it or not, many employers believe that past behavior predicts future behavior. The best way for them to predict how you will perform on a new job is to look at how you performed on past jobs.

That's why many interviewers like the behavior descriptive interview. Simply stated, you will be asked to provide snippets of your past to show how you performed a task and what the outcome was. There are a number of good resources on this type of interview.

You may be asked a number of questions that begin, 'When in the past did you...'.

The best way to prepare for such interviews is to think of a number of difficult situations you had on past jobs that turned out well due to some action on your part. You've got to prepare well for this type of interview.

Even if the interview is not a behavior descriptive one, the preparation will be good for other kinds of interviews as well.

Deal with their fears about hiring an older worker.

What are some of those fears?

- You're just too old to catch on to new procedures (like computer stuff)

- You can't keep up the pace a younger worker can

- You wouldn't take direction from a younger (sometimes much younger) boss

- You will only stay in this job until something better comes along

- You are going to retire soon

Ask yourself, are any of these true? If they're not, in what ways are you going to reassure an employer?

Example: 'I'm current with my computer skills and haven't had any problems completing my work on time and accurately'.

Okay, now what are the pluses of hiring a mature worker?

- Life experience

- Experience making decisions and knowing what the outcomes will be

- Good work ethic, calls in sick only when sick, schedules personal appointments outside of work hours whenever possible, etc.

- Sets a good example for younger workers

How will you fit in?

Each workplace is a distinct 'family' of employees. Part of the interview process is discovering whether you'd fit in this family.

You may or may not have inside knowledge about what the family is like. In any case, don't try to guess. Let your own personality come through in an interview.

Think about it. If they hire you based on what you pretend to be, they'll discover the real you soon enough. But if they hire the real you, you can feel more confident that it is a good fit.

Role play for the camera.

You might be thinking, 'That's so Eighties!'. But role playing--that is, practicing how you will answer typical interview questions with a partner--makes sense.

In the olden days we career counselors would film a person in this role play. The day before, I told each workshop participant to dress appropriately and act exactly as though they were going to an interview when they came in the next day.

We had a video camera pointed at them from the moment they walked in the door, not just on the interview itself. When we played it back, most of the people were surprised, some were shocked.

'Do I really come across like that?' was the typical response.

Even today with all the social media, you'd think we have a good idea of how we present ourselves to the world. But few of us know how we look and act in an interview. At the least, have your role play partner ask you a few of the toughest questions.

Is your voice a monotone? Do you fiddle with your hair or talk (maybe shout) with your hands? Do you avoid eye contact? Maybe you didn't smile once. This is the way an interviewer sees you.

In less than a minute of viewing yourself on camera you can make some crucial changes to your personal presentation.

How many people will you be facing?
When you get the call for the actual interview you could ask who will be present. If it will make you more nervous to know, don't ask.

One-to-one interviews are getting rare. They usually happen when you are applying for a job in a small business where the owner can make most of the decisions and trusts their own judgment to hire the right person.

There might be two interviewers or several (panel interview). It can be intimidating to face a boardroom full of people in an interview. Don't assume that everyone there is a crackerjack interviewer ready to grill you under hot lights, however. Sometimes employees from various departments get hauled in to the boardroom a minute before the interview just to fill the seats. They might have very little knowledge of the position you're applying for.

It's been my experience that no matter how many people are there, it's usually only one or two people who are dominant in the interview. They will likely be sitting close to your right and your left. Most of the others will be taking notes or they might be allowed to ask the odd question. It can feel strange to have several people all writing down their interpretation of your answers.

No matter how many people are in the room, try to make eye contact with each of them once during the interview — even if just for a few seconds. Suddenly you are not just another task in their day. You are a person. You'll often see the little surprise in their eyes as you make that eye contact.

Be friendly and treat everyone with respect. But it's the big guns to your left and right who will likely be driving the interview, setting the pace and the tone.

This is a two-way street.

Just as they're trying to decide if you would be good for their company, you are deciding if the job and company would be good for you. Ever been on an interview where you thought, 'This is never gonna work'? You complete the interview, politely thank them for their time, and walk out the door never to return.

The day of the interview

Of course you've checked the route, available parking, etc. Also, have their phone number in case you're held up for reasons beyond your control.

As soon as you walk into the parking lot of the building where your interview is, have a smile for everyone you see. You don't know who they are at this point—that could be the president of the company getting into her car.

Once you get to reception, be especially polite. Bosses may ask their front line staff for comments on your attitude, behavior, etc. (They could also be doing this if you drop off your resume in person.)

Now that you're inside and waiting to be called in for the interview, panic can set in. You might be thinking—I have to get this job. No, you don't. You need a job, that's true, but this might not be the one.

Tell yourself that you've prepared as well as you could, you will do your best in the interview, and then you will let it go. There are factors beyond your control here.

Interview Outfits  10

Know your field. Is it conservative, creative, or something in between?

Then choose your outfit accordingly. You'll want to dress 'up' from what you might see current employees wearing. People tend to become lax about dress codes the longer they are in a job.

In general, start with clean, classic styles. If one of your fears is they will think you're too old for the job or won't fit in, then:

Add something new and a little trendy to your interview outfit.

To a conservative suit, add a new tie with a pattern that's in style. You can get one of your adult kids to help pick out that one stylish touch, a touch that tells the employer that you are adaptable. It says you may be mature but you're open to new ideas, you've kept up with the times. A woman might wear small scarf that adds a splash of color to that conservative outfit, or a trendy bracelet.

You don't want to make drastic changes just before important interviews. Just add a touch or two that's still inside your comfort zone.

Forget about going on a shopping spree. That's not likely what you need or can afford right now. Go through your wardrobe and weed out the things that don't make you feel good when you wear them. Make small repairs to your favorite duds so that everything's ready at a moment's notice.

Comfortable and confident

You've got to feel comfortable and confident in what you're wearing. You know it's the right outfit when you put it on and forget about it.

Your 'best' outfit might not be the right one for a job interview. We often buy our best clothes based on how they look, not how they feel. If you're worried that the pants are too clingy, or something is too tight and will show those extra ten pounds, or you know you will be tugging at the too-short sleeves—then it's not the right outfit.

You don't need to be worrying about your clothes. You'll have enough on your mind today.

Have a couple of good interview outfits ready at all times.

You never know when someone will call you up and say, "Can you drop in for a few minutes today? This isn't a formal interview, but our district manager just happens to be in today and was looking over your resume. . ."

So have a couple of complete outfits ready to throw on at a moment's notice, right down to the socks you'll wear. Carry a couple of safety pins and maybe one of those instant laundry pens as well. Remember Murphy's Law? Murphy just loves job interviews.

What about my appearance? Do I look my age or older?

Take a good look at yourself in the mirror. Are you confident with the way you look? If you are, it will show. Don't change a thing.

But maybe you think you could use a few changes. I'm not suggesting Botox here. And gray hair is a personal choice. It's not so much how you look but how you think about how you look.

And that's the secret.

Having said that, a few changes might lift your spirits, something you likely need during an intense job hunt.

A new haircut is a great investment. If you're on a tight budget consider going to a beauty school where students cut your hair under strict supervision.

A trusted friend might give you some surprising suggestions for improvements.

What do I bring?

I try to leave my coat at reception if possible. Then I have a simple black portfolio—big enough to hold an 8 ½ by 10 notepad, a couple of pens, extra copies of my resume, copies of my reference page, sticky notes. That's what's comfortable for me. You don't want to appear like you've brought a set of luggage with all the fixings for a magic show inside.

And know exactly where everything is. Rifling through a pile of papers can make you look disorganized and unprepared.

But that's not going to happen to you. You've done your preparation so you can concentrate on what you will say.

Interview Questions

11

What's the real question?

Every interview question is really asking, 'Why should we hire you for this position?'. At the end of the interview, when they add up the pluses and minuses, this is really the question they will be asking themselves.

No one wants to be known for hiring someone who eventually had to be fired. They want to pick a winner. You can help them. You can answer their unspoken plea: Please give me great reasons to hire you instead of one of the four people waiting in reception.

Prove it.

Whenever you talk about your experience, prove it. "I have a clean safety record and won the department award three years running" or "My previous employer commented on my ability to adapt to changes on the job, on my performance appraisal".

Even when asked a hypothetical question, give an example from your past. When they ask, "What would you do if — ", give an actual example where this happened to you and there was a positive outcome. For example, "How would you handle conflict with a co-worker?"

"This happened in one of my past jobs. A co-worker and I didn't seem to be communicating at first. I knew that our work could be affected by this, so I met with him alone in his office and asked what I could do to improve the situation. . . The outcome was that we agreed to co-ordinate our efforts better and plan our schedules around key issues. We're still friends today."

You have to prepare for these. Have in mind a few examples from your past where there was a problem and it was resolved. Things like — disagreement with a co-worker, how you handled stress at work, ethical things.

Spend most of your time practicing answers to the questions you know will give you the most trouble.

Like some kind of weird radar, employers seem to have an uncanny sense of asking the questions you'd rather avoid. I picture an antennae strapped to their heads. Don't make the mistake of not preparing your answers to the tough questions.

Make a list of the questions that you don't want to answer, with the scariest ones at the top.

Do you feel confident that these past situations wouldn't affect this new job? Why? Note that whenever possible, you will apply for jobs where this situation would not be an issue.

For example, if you were fired, why were you fired? The interviewer may frame it as 'Why did you leave your last employment?'.

To prepare for this question, ask yourself honestly, why were you fired?

What actually happened there? Was it just a bad match between you and the job? Was it something about you, like always being late? And do you think the same situation might well come up in this new job?

If it's something about you, like being late, what steps have you taken to remedy the situation? If past behavior predicts future behavior, will you always be late in this new job?

If you don't feel confident in your own answer to yourself, then you can bet the interviewer's radar will be on high alert. Think twice about applying for jobs where the past may come back to bite you.

So:

Why did you leave your last employment?
If you quit a job:

'My last job involved shift work. I started work in the late afternoon. I discovered that this schedule didn't work for me, so that's why I decided to look for work from 8 a.m. to 5 p.m. so I could have more time with my family.'

Of course you are now applying for a job that doesn't involve shift work. It just wouldn't make sense to apply for jobs where the past problem might repeat itself.

There's usually more than one reason to quit a job. You may not have got along with the supervisor, the money was poor, it might have been a long commute to work or (fill in the blank).

There are big red flags to an employer: Not getting along with a past supervisor is one of them. The interviewer wants to know if you have a history of problems with the boss. If that's the case, he's afraid the same thing will happen if he hired you for his company.

So if you have several reasons for leaving a job, you can choose to name one that is more 'acceptable'. For example, you are looking for a better wage. Most employers can understand that.

'I needed to make more money, and just one of the reasons I've applied for this job is that I know that your company is competitive with standard industry wages'.

This is a grey area and everyone must follow their own conscience. Take a good look at this new job. Do you think the past will repeat itself there? Then keep looking.

If you've been laid off you might still be bitter about it and justifiably so. But you still had to put that job on your resume because it's relevant to the jobs you're seeking now.

But wait a minute. All the interviewer sees is your anger. Your bad memories about that job will show in your face.

No one wants to hire an angry person. They expect you to leave that baggage at the door of your old workplace no matter how painful it was.

You're going to have to practice what you'll say about that old job, that old boss, and that old company. You have to get to a point where the emotion is not obvious. Practice in front of a mirror until you get it. You're aiming for a professional tone. A touch of regret, perhaps, that such decisions must occasionally be made. But you have moved on with renewed optimism.

I usually tell the interviewer that I was laid off and that I was assured that it was a business decision that had nothing to do with my work performance.

My thoughts might be saying something a little less kind. I might not like it, I might hate the fact that I was let go. But in interviews I've learned to be professional even when my inner child is kicking and screaming.

You might detest that last employer for what they did to you and your family. But don't let them control your future. The best revenge is success.

How old are you?

Questions about age, marital status, race, religion, etc. are illegal, but many interviewers ask outright or ask in a roundabout way. Some interviewers don't know it's illegal. Others just don't care and ask anyway.

Sooner or later you'll be asked an illegal question. You're sitting there in the boardroom or office of a potential employer wondering how on earth you can avoid answering this question. You have a few choices here.

Yes, you absolutely have rights and don't have to answer illegal questions. Yes, you can point this out to the employer in a nice way. Or you can stand up and declare your rights and walk out. But chances are you won't get that job.

I like to assume that the interviewer is just not up on the legalities. All things being equal, if it's a good job and the questions have been normal so far, I don't take offence. I try to look at the reason they might be asking the question.

The fear behind the question: 'We had to let another older worker go because he just couldn't keep up with the technology'.

Possible answer: 'If you're concerned about my computer skills. . ." (tell them how you've kept up-to-date with the latest software in your industry).

Tell me about yourself.

They don't want to know about how you skinned your knee in the driveway when you were eight. Again, that good old word 'relevant' should be floating in front of your eyes.

You can start off by saying something like, 'I was born and raised here in the Northwest. Very soon after completing college, I began working in widget management and haven't looked back'.

You have quickly steered the topic to answer the question: Why you for this job?. That's what you're here to do.

Then you will modestly but confidently (yes, that takes practice) go over your achievements that are most relevant to the job you are applying for.

You can also mention your career plans for the future if you feel they are a good match to this job. Be careful of this one, though. Too many people talk themselves out of a job at this point.

What would your last employer say about you?

To prepare for this question, ask yourself what she really would say about you. Even if you were let go, there are probably some good things she would say.

'I believe she would say that I was an overall asset to the department, especially in the areas of team building and morale."

What did you dislike about your last job?

What is the fear behind this question? The employer fears that the things you hated about your last job could be repeated at this job. Note that this question could be phrased as: What are your weaknesses?

To prepare for this question, be honest with yourself. What things do you really dislike doing? Then find out if you would be doing that a lot on this new job. Before you apply you should feel confident that it doesn't have the same elements you disliked at the old place. Or if you were laid off and really loved your job, then this new one can give you the opportunity to continue doing something you love.

Then, how to answer it? You don't want to come across as putting down either the job or your last employer. You don't want to sound Pollyanna-ish, either.

Here's a balanced reply: 'Like with any job, there are things that you like to do more than others. But if the job is to be done well, you have to look at all your responsibilities and do them to the best of your ability. I am always looking for ways to improve my skills'.

If they keep pressing for specifics, pick a couple of things that are not in the top four essential elements in the job you're applying for: 'General reception duties are not my strong point. My strength lies in one-to-one contact with the client. Although I'd be glad to step in and answer phones in a pinch, it wouldn't be something that I would want to do all day.'

How do you handle conflict?
There are variations on this question, like, 'Tell me a time when you've had a disagreement with a co-worker'.

They want to know how you get along. Do you play nicely with others?

We all have had conflicts with co-workers at times. Some may be minor things like failing to share information. Maybe once in your life there was a major personality clash when one of you had to go.

The best way to prepare for this question is to think up a few conflicts in the past that were resolved in a good way. That's why preparing for questions like this is so important. You have to think of a problem, yes, but a problem that was resolved where you were part of the solution.

Whenever possible, answer the question with a specific case without naming the company or co-workers involved.

'Several years ago I faced a situation where a colleague in another department wasn't passing on important information I needed to do my job. After several attempts to call and email him, I went to his office and quietly knocked on the door. We were able to discuss the problem calmly, just the two of us. It turned out that he had several concerns about sharing his department's information. After we addressed each of those concerns we arranged to meet once a week to update each other.'

This showed that you recognized the problem and dealt with it in a calm, quiet manner. It also shows respect for one's colleagues by communicating your concerns in private. And there was no blame attached—you acknowledge that it could have been a misunderstanding. The bottom line—you cleared it up so that the work could get done.

Employers want to know that you can be a problem solver, not a problem maker. That doesn't mean you have to be a pushover, far from it. You treat others with respect and expect the same.

How do you handle stress?

The question behind this question: Will you be able to handle the stress on this job?

They often ask it because past employees have found the job itself or something in the work environment to be stressful. This can be a heads-up that this job might be more stressful than you bargained on.

They want to know that you have healthy ways of dealing with stress as opposed to taking out your frustrations on colleagues or customers, taking drugs, or any number of inappropriate things.

This question could be another way of asking how you handle conflict with co-workers or clients.

With any question you can ask for clarification: 'Do you mean daily stress on the job, or stress in general?'. You may not get that clarification.

What healthy ways do you use to combat stress? Regular work-outs at the gym, a daily walk at lunch, yoga, a healthy diet?

If you've had a similar job in the past, you can say that you were able to handle the stress well (if that's true of course).

Where do you see yourself two (or three, or five) years from now?

They could be looking for a number of things here. They might be putting a hook in the water to see just what fish they'll pull up.

You could take this question to mean that they're asking about your commitment to the field. Do you really love health care and can see yourself doing this for at least the next five years? Then say so.

Another question behind this question might be: 'How old are you? Are you almost ready for retirement?'. The 'R' word is not one I use in interviews. They don't want to hire someone who is planning to go out the back door soon after they've let them in the front. Instead, I give an energetic plan for my future, which of course revolves around the industry I'm applying for. And it's got to be true.

It can also tell them a lot more about you. Do you even have a five-year plan for your life? Have you thought that far ahead?

What salary would you expect?

They might be afraid that someone with your qualifications is just too expensive for them.

You don't want to give a figure during the job interview. Period. If you are really pressed, that is, if they come back to the question one or more times (see Boomerang Questions), you can give them a broad range of what you would want (and of course you've done your research into what kind of salary you might be able to expect at this job).

A job interview usually isn't the place for hardball salary negotiations. Think about it. Whatever figure you give them won't be right. Say you tell them you'd take $50,000. They have in their minds that they could go as high as $55,000. Sure they'll take you for five thousand less. And you might never know that you lost five thousand dollars in five minutes.

Or say you tell them you want $60,000. They throw up their hands, thinking you're way too expensive. It's another way to eliminate you from the competition.

You might, by a stroke of chance, guess right on to what they're thinking. Maybe their magic number is $52,000. That's the number they have in their heads as you are walking through the door of the interview.

But wait a minute. Now that you're here in person to expand on your skills and achievements, they may be changing that number in their minds as they speak to you. So now they're willing to offer you $55,000 or maybe even more.

So you can see that giving any kind of specific number in an interview just doesn't make sense.

Instead, say something like, 'I'm confident that after you review my unique qualifications for this job that we can come to a mutual agreement on salary'. And add a mysterious little smile.

Have in mind that broad range that you will give them if you're absolutely forced to, but avoid giving it nonetheless.

Once you have a firm job offer, you are in a better position to negotiate. They are saying that you are the one they want above all the others. And they are nervously waiting to see if they can afford you.

Do you have any questions for us?

Well, do you? Are there things you're dying to know that your research couldn't tell you?

One of my favorite questions to ask them is, 'A year from now, how will you know you hired the right person?'.

I've been given pat answers like 'From their annual performance review'. But I've also been given a few key points that may not have been brought up so far, something in the interviewer's head that may never have come to light until now.

'I'll know we've hired the right person when all our clients get jobs.'

It may be intended as a light answer, but this is your chance to—briefly—name a couple of your accomplishments in that area. Remember, it's the end of the interview and you want to be concise.

Boomerang Questions

You thought you answered the question. But a few minutes later, they ask it again in another form. Either they didn't get the answer they were looking for the first time around, or it's a very important subject for them, or both. Like, how you get along with co-workers. This could signal that they've had problems with workers in the past and they want to be darned sure that you won't be part of the problem if they hire you.

So make sure they are satisfied with your answer this time. Answer it, and then ask if they would like you to give details.

When you think all is lost...

I once tried to prepare for a job by stuffing my head with lists of facts about the position and the organization, like cramming for the biggest exam of my life. There were a couple of major distractions right before the interview and guess what, all that stored information in my head dissolved. When faced with questions about their many programs and services, I couldn't remember a thing.

I had to admit that I couldn't remember. You would think that all was lost at that point.

So I told them my philosophy. When a client came through my door, I treated him like a human being, the way I would want to be treated. He may have a criminal record, or have been rejected by other agencies, but for the moment, when he came through my door, he would have someone to listen. I wouldn't be madly tapping his information into a computer. I wanted to make eye contact, human contact. I wanted to have some uninterrupted time when I asked him what brought him here.

It worked. It turned out that my philosophy matched theirs.

Let YOU show in an interview.

Sure, you want the job, and heaven knows you need a job. But you also want it to be a good match. It won't do you any good to fake it by twisting yourself into a pretzel to match yourself to the job, only to find out in a month that it was a really bad decision.

If you feel really strongly about something, let it show. If you can't bear to be micro-managed, you might say that while you get along well on teams, you are also an independent worker. A boss can be assured that when he hires you, you can do your job without constant supervision.

If he's a micro-manager, he won't hire you. That's a good thing.

End on a good note

Take the interviewer's cue that the interview is over.

Smile, shake hands, thank them for their time. And say you want this job. Not in a desperate kind of way, but in a positive way—if you really mean it.

Post Interview

If you're like most people, the moment you walk out the door of the interview you may be beating yourself up over questions you didn't quite get, or a key point you forgot to mention about your experience. We all do it.

Don't sweat it.

You prepared as well as you could given your present circumstances (which usually involves some minor household emergency the night before or the morning of), so don't put yourself down. You're human. You did the best you could. Let it go.

That takes some practice but you get better at it. Make a note of things you could improve for the future but the past is just that—over, gonzo. And five minutes ago is in the past.

A mini celebration is called for.

Give yourself a little treat for having gone through the interview. That may be picking up a specialty coffee on the way home or taking a nice long walk to unwind. Make this a scheduled thing you do for yourself no matter how badly (you think) the interview went. Come to think of it, you especially need it then.

If job hunting is your new job, then getting through an interview, especially an intense one, is the same as completing a tough presentation on any job.

Be nice to yourself. You did good.

A note about Thank You notes

Some people swear by them, others feel they're a little contrived. It's a personal choice. If you do send a thank-you note to the interviewers use a plain business style, no fluffy flowers or kittens.

If you are using a hand-delivered thank-you note as a selling tool to help them make a decision, mention a couple of things that will remind them of the interview. For example, 'Thank you for your time and consideration. I was especially interested in your new product line which is a great match to the one I was recently managing. . .'

How long do I have to wait for an answer?

Before you leave the interview you can ask when they will be making a decision. It might be anywhere from a few hours to two weeks. That could be even longer if you are close to a holiday when people who make those decisions will be away.

While you're waiting, keep busy with your job search. Make a note of a few things you might improve for your next interview.

Call them on the day they said they'll make their decision. Even if the answer is 'no', you can still thank them for the opportunity and say you would be very interested in working for them in the future. You could inquire about future job openings.

You can ask them what points you might improve on. Some companies won't comment. But others will give you valuable feedback. The feedback might surprise you.

This conversation will tell them a lot about you. They will expect you to be disappointed, of course, but you will accept their decision with grace like the professional person you are. And plant the seed of doubt that maybe they hired the wrong person.

It has been known that a person might quit soon after they were hired or that things don't work out and some mutual agreement is made where the person leaves or is offered a different job. In that case, the company may give you a call.

Or maybe you were not the person they wanted for the advertised position, but you made such an impression on them that you are offered another position in the company. These things happen more often than you think. That's why you want to remain on excellent terms with them.

The Patchwork Quilt Economy

You may be holding out for a full-time job. But sometimes there just aren't that many out there.

Would you consider doing a couple of part-time jobs? Add on a temporary contract, some work-at-home projects?

It can be tricky to juggle two or more things at once, but there's a virtual Santa's sack of advantages:

It keeps you busy.

It gets you out of the house, or even if you are working from home, you have a work schedule again. It's amazing what that does for one's self esteem.

It brings in income.

Another big boost to your self-esteem, not to mention your Piggy Bank. After being laid off from my main job, it was a small but lucrative contract I'd been doing on the side that paid my bills.

You will have experience to add to your resume.

One of the big things about being out of work is that it creates a gap in your resume. But not if you've stayed active by working on projects. You show future employers that you are not the type to let grass grow under your feet.

It can give you current references.

This is especially good if you can't use your last supervisor as a reference for the 'big' jobs coming up.

It can show future employers that you are adaptable.

Employers know the job situation: Many people are out of work. They also know that life is not so much about what happens to you, it's about what you are doing to improve your situation. And taking on two or three projects or jobs can show that you are a hard worker. You can adapt to bad times and keep your optimism. People admire that.

It can be a chance to explore your two passions and make valuable connections.

You could explore one or two of your passions by taking on short-term projects. And the best part of it is, you will be paid to do something you love. You would actually (shhhh) pay them for this opportunity!

It gives you the chance to try new skills.

An employer who is looking for a full-time employee has a lot at stake. It can feel like everyone in the company is watching to see who the perfect candidate will be. You might feel like you'll never meet that high bar.

But a small contract? The employer may be willing to give you a chance, even if you don't have all the skills to do the job yet.

It gives you the chance to try out a few companies to see if you would like working for one on a more permanent basis.

I once worked as a temp. When I was assigned to an employer I didn't especially like, I knew that the term would soon end. And when I found a great employer, neither one of us wanted to part. So they 'bought out' my contract with the temp agency and hired me on a permanent, full-time basis.

Just to show you how much wheeling and dealing goes on in the employment world, the cost of buying me out of the contract was prohibitive. It was designed to discourage companies from doing exactly this--poaching the temp workers from the agency. But my future employer told them, not so subtly, that if the agency wanted their continued business, they would waive the fee. Instantly done.

It can get your toe in the door to a great opportunity.

By starting with an organization with a temporary contract or part-time position, the employer has a chance to sit back and watch your performance before they invest a full-time salary in you. They might not have realized that there was a full-time job there, but when the end of your contract comes, they just don't want to let you go.

It can get you past that 'older worker' label when they see what you can do.

If someone has doubts about you based on your age (not that they'll tell you) but has hired you part time to start, this is your time to shine. You'll bust all those outdated notions they have about age when they see how you perform on the job.

You have become the problem-solver, a great position to be in.

Short-term contracts often mean that the employer needs someone in a pinch. You saved the day. That's a great way to start a business relationship.

All of this might sound like a lot of work in itself, especially if you've had a full-time job for a number of years. But even when you had that job, weren't there days when you dreamed about trying something different?

Keep an open mind about this patchwork quilt economy. One of the reasons you're reading this book is likely because the old way of finding traditional jobs hasn't worked for you.

So take the plunge. What do you have to lose?

Me? An Entrepreneur?

14

Consider being your own boss.

You might be sitting on a hefty severance package or you might be surviving on a shoestring. Should you start a business?

That depends. Have you always had the urge to be your own boss?

Did you make things and sell them to the neighborhood kids when you were young?

Do you watch programs and read about inventors and start-up businesses?

When you see a new product or service are you thinking, 'I could do that better'?

Does the thought of having yet another boss somehow rankle you?

Business ownership is NOT for everyone. If you've never had a thought about owning one until you lost your last job, then have a serious talk with yourself. Will all thoughts of being an entrepreneur evaporate the minute you get a job offer?

If that's the case, then that's what you should be doing—looking for a job instead of starting a business.

But if you know that your dreams of a business will never die no matter what job you have to take on to keep peanut butter on the table, then yes, you might be a born entrepreneur.

Think outside the box. Literally.

When you think of owning a business, do you picture having a store on Main Street with several employees? Or a big box store on the outskirts of town?

That's only one way to have your own business. Today there are many options for being your own boss.

You might be the only employee. You might provide a service from your basement office. Maybe you'll never see a customer or client in person. As in the case of freelance writing, I rarely meet editors in person. Usually I write at home, send the finished piece via email, and get a cheque in the mail.

What service or product would you provide, and to whom?

Maybe you've been thinking about this for years and have perfected your product in your mind. If not, look around your town. What service have you wanted for yourself and couldn't get? Would you want to provide that service for others? Or think of the product you were trying to find online. It doesn't exist. At least, not yet.

Businesses nowadays come in many forms. You might provide a small translation business out of your home. You might sell products on the Net to your customers in Europe.

Start some serious research. Draft a plan.

Play. Make sketches. Dream. Close your eyes and picture it like a movie you've walked into. What are you doing? Where? Set the scene.

What does your business look like? Where do you see it in two years?

Now open your eyes and put foundations under that dream. What would it take to start? Can you do this business out of your home? The possibilities should stream in.

Once you have a good idea of where you're going, talk to people who are doing it.

Interview for information.

People usually like to share what they know. They were once in the position you are now: Green, green as a baby leaf.

Like with cold calls, you are bound to get a few people who don't want to talk to you. Fine. There's plenty of fish in the sea. And many of those fish will talk.

You can also email people. It's surprising how many important people will email you, even if it might be impossible to get through to them by phone. That's partly because they can reply to your email at their convenience. Check the website of the company for email addresses.

The key to successful information interviews is number one, Respect. You are respectful of the person's time and expertise. You will do more listening than talking yourself.

Keep in mind that if you want to open a small bakery for example, talking to another small baker in your town might not be a great idea. They will see you as potential competition. So, talk to a small baker in a town out of your region, but one that faces similar laws and regulations.

There will be questions you don't even know to ask right now. The person who has been there will tell you what they are.

If you can at least take them out for a coffee while you're talking, so much the better. The advice they are offering could be worth thousands to you down the road.

When you go after the things you love and do well, good things start to happen. Opportunities open up. Maybe not today, but you'll start to see progress in your life.

Sample questions for your information interview:

In any kind of interview, go in with an open mind. Don't anticipate the answers. You're there to learn something.

You'll have specific questions but you also want to ask some open-ended ones that will give you answers you'd never expect:

- ♦ What do you do in a typical day (and how long is a typical day)?

- ♦ Where do you see the business in a year? In two years?

- ♦ How do you know when it's a smart time to invest more money in any aspect of the business?

- ♦ Do you still see yourself doing this in five years? Why? Why not?

- ♦ Is this the ideal business for you? What would you have done differently starting out?

- ♦ What is the biggest question I should be asking, starting out?

Start small.

Being over 50, you may be trying to hold on to what you've managed to put away for retirement. Starting small with your entrepreneurial dreams, on a part-time basis from home, is one way to minimize risk. You could still work at an outside job to support your family.

The other end of the scale would be to open a store in a great location with employees to manage. If that's your choice, you will have done it only after extensive research.

Even then, there are no guarantees. It comes down to how much you're willing to risk.

The true entrepreneur will go ahead with their plans after considering the risk. Life is short and uncertain anyway—didn't you just find that out after losing your job?

There's something exciting about having your own business, even if it's just something on the side. There's the old story from communist Russia where farmers had to work on the communal farm but were each allowed one small plot of land to grow their own crops for market. The production on that small plot soared compared to the land they were forced to farm. Long live the free enterprise system.

A few ideas for small enterprises for the over 50:

<u>Bookkeeper from home (but with a twist)</u>: Again, think of two passions you could combine and look around and match that to potential customers. You love horses. Could you provide bookkeeping for everything from riding stables to tack shops?

<u>Freelance writer:</u> First, you have to be a good writer. Then start with topics you love. Then find the markets that will pay the most for that writing. You may have to write a few articles for free to build up your writing credits—but don't do too many for free.

Non-fiction articles will likely pay you the most, as opposed to writing a novel which can take more than a year and has a ghost of a chance of getting accepted by a publisher. You might consider writing a Print On Demand book like this one.

Would you be considered an expert in some area? Rock climbing? Travelling with four small children? Look at your passions again. Then think of an article you'd like to write and contact the editors of publications you love to read (print and online) — by email, if possible--with a short proposal (two or three paragraphs of the specific topic, who you would interview, etc).

There should be very low start-up costs for freelance writing. In the olden days, stamps were a big expense. But with the magic of email things are faster and cheaper.

The downside is that freelance writing can take some time to start paying well. You need time to develop a good business relationship with a few editors from lucrative markets. Someone who loves your writing and considers you a professional. That means getting the article in on time and generally being polite and cooperative when they suggest changes.

<u>Plumber sitter:</u> How many times have you heard someone groan when they have to wait all day for a service person to come to their home? Ever notice that it's hard to pin them down to even morning or afternoon? Many people lose work hours because they have to be home to let in the plumber, the cable guy, the person who repairs the elliptical machine, etc. But you could do this for them. You let the repair person in and make sure the cat doesn't escape at the same time. This is a good sideline if you have

something else to do while they work–like writing your next freelance article, for example.

Assembler: Ever go into a box store and want to buy the fancy whatzit only to discover you have to assemble it yourself? What's that all about? Just add water? Or what about all those toys around Christmas time? Or stereo systems, or new TV hook-ups?

If you love putting things together, there are many more people who hate putting things together. You could leave your business card at local stores. You could do this independently or arrange something with the store. It could be a good business decision for them to provide this service for their customers, for a fee.

Haul it: As I write this, I can't find one person with a pick-up truck to haul some extra furniture to the local Salvation Army Thrift Store. I'd gladly pay to have someone do this and declutter the house. Or deliver a new couch from a store to home. You could provide this service.

Volunteer!  15

You can gain many of the same benefits from the Patchwork Quilt Economy if you volunteer.

So why would you volunteer your time for free when you could be earning a little dough?

You might be in a temporary slump with your job hunt. You've applied all over and are doing everything you should. But at the moment nothing is happening. You could spare an hour or so to volunteer.

You call the shots.

I'm not talking about canvassing for money door to door for a cause, unless that's your passion. I'm talking about volunteering to gain experience and contacts doing something you love.

If you're volunteering, you should be doing something with one of your passions. Exactly what kind of experience do you want, and where? What hours are convenient for you? One morning a week? Since you're volunteering you should be able to call the shots.

That's what I did. Having lost a job due to a move for a better opportunity for my spouse (and ultimately for both of us), I was left staring at four walls. I needed human contact. I was actively job hunting but sometimes the wheels move very slowly in the employment world.

I always loved history, especially postcards and old photos. Wouldn't it be great if there was a job out there that let me look at dozens of them all day?

Nah. No way. My new city wasn't exactly a huge metropolis. The odds of there even being a job like that were slim to none.

So I approached the local archives. I told them I loved old photos and history. It turns out that many original photos were quickly disintegrating. The more people who handled them, the faster this process went.

But when copies of the photos can be accessed from a computer, the originals can stay safe and happy in their acid-free envelopes. So the archives people quickly showed me to a scanner where I began digitally scanning hundreds of old photos.

They couldn't get a volunteer to stick with a scanning project for long. For most people, sitting at a desk and scanning photos all day is deadly dull.

Then along came me and far from finding it dull, I was ecstatic. Imagine being allowed to look at all those old photos, to see history from the street level, to snoop into the lives of people a hundred years ago! And I would be helping to preserve history for the next generations.

I don't think that even the archives people could see why I was so excited about doing the scanning project. One day the boss—much younger than me, by the way (not that there's anything wrong with that)—brought me into his office. I was offered a contract to scan more photos. Not only were they going to pay me for something I'd willingly do for free, they were going to pay Big Bucks.

There was more to it than that. While I was volunteering the management noticed that I got along with the staff, showed up on time, and worked hard. I made a note of how many photos I could scan in a day and each day I competed with my old best record. I treated that volunteer position as seriously as any job. So they hired me.

Volunteering is a great way to build experience, contacts, new skills. And when a new position comes up, lots of organizations feel honor bound to at least consider their volunteers. Make it known that you are thrilled to volunteer, but you'd appreciate it if they inform you of job openings as well.

Keeps your resume current.

As with part-time work or contracts, volunteer experience can keep your resume current. I list all my experience, paid or unpaid, under the heading Relevant Experience and treat the volunteer position as a job where I gained valuable skills.

Another success story

Since volunteering my way to a job worked so well, I often tell other people about it. I'm always a little amazed when someone follows my advice and it takes off in ways neither of us could predict.

A friend had always wanted to work in a library but thought that her lack of a degree would prevent it. I suggested she volunteer for a children's program at the local library.

She loved it and they loved her. Although there were no positions available in that library, within weeks she used the experience and excellent references gained from volunteering to get a very good job at another library. She sings her way to work each morning, not quite believing that her dream has come true.

My friend, by going with her passions, stood out because few people could match that energy. People could see that she's not just good with children and libraries—she truly has a gift for both.

When you volunteer doing something you absolutely love, that passion shows. Little things don't bug you. Time flies. You're willing to go the distance, do a little extra, and learn all you can because you love it. People respond to that.

Volunteering can help you adapt to change.

When you volunteer, you open yourself up to new experiences and new people. If you were in your last job for years, you need this. Once you start a new job you'll be leaving your comfort zone about a hundred miles behind. Volunteering can help prepare you for this.

One of the best things you can work on is your ability to adapt to change. Volunteering puts you in different settings working with people and situations you may never have encountered before.

Volunteering can give you valuable training for free.

I learned about digital photos, websites, and scanners on the archives job, not to mention archival procedures. If I had applied for a paid job they would have expected me to know all this. But as a volunteer, they knew they would have to teach me certain aspects of the technology.

A funny thing about technology. Once they get to know you and like you, you'll often find that your co-workers are more than willing to help you with a computer glitch or a new procedure. That doesn't mean you're dragging someone away from their desk every five minutes. You are expected to know the basics of your job. But when people like you, they help you. And of course you'll do the same for them in other areas.

Offer a free trial period.

Maybe you've contacted an employer during your job search and they are a little hesitant about accepting your resume. They might talk vaguely about recent budget cuts in their department. They might be concerned about any number of things. Maybe it's about your age and maybe it isn't.

Offer to volunteer on a small project for them. If they like what they see you might be offered a job.

People don't like strangers.

That's why it's so hard to get a job by just sending a cover letter and resume. Lots of people lie on those things. But when a boss sees how well you work and how well you interact with their staff, you are no longer a stranger. And if they like you, they will be reluctant to let you go. Don't be surprised if a paid opportunity suddenly becomes available just before your volunteer hours are complete.

Note: If you are on unemployment insurance, check to see if they would consider your time volunteering as 'unavailable to work' and possibly disqualify you.

Connect with other Earthlings

Connect with people each day.
Isolation is the kiss of death for job hunters. Even introverts need people contact during the course of the day.

Join a job club, volunteer, or take on a series of small projects. If for nothing else, do it to have a reason to get dressed in the morning. You will feel better for it.

If you can, make some time—maybe just a coffee in the morning—to connect with friends. It gives your family a break from trying to boost your spirits. They are under pressure, too.

A friend is a supportive person you trust who doesn't have a financial stake in your job search. They can look at your situation with neutral eyes and maybe give you some good advice.

Stay in contact with friends, don't feel ashamed. And yes, you'll have to face the questions—Have you found work yet?, etc. But being with friends can be such good medicine that it's worth fielding a few snoopy but well-meaning questions.

No matter how supportive a spouse and family can be, they need you to get back to work. That's a lot of pressure on all of you.

Friends don't have that kind of expectation. After an occasional day out with the boys or girls, you will often come back home with a sense of renewal, that life is not so grim. You had a few laughs. You enjoyed yourself. You needed that.

But don't forget your family. You likely haven't been a barrel of laughs lately. Plan some family silly time — a water fight in the backyard, a pillow fight, whatever you normally do to let off steam.

Learn to accept help.

We Boomers have a lot of pride. We don't like to ask for help. But that's basically what a successful job search is, asking for help.

Do you think ultra-successful people got where they're at all alone? Check out the biography of a famous person you admire. Make a mental list of all the people who helped along the way. No one succeeds in a vacuum.

You are going to get back on your feet again, and the way you're going to do it is — someone is going to help you. Probably several people are going to help you.

It may be a former co-worker who gives you a lead on a job. An old friend who suggests a place you can rent cheap. A new acquaintance whose spouse works in your industry. Someone will like what they see in you and give you an opportunity. It's your connection with other Earthlings that's going to get you back in the game.

Charity? Not at all. We all need help at times, and the truth is, people like to help. It makes them feel good. Let them feel good by helping you. You'll pay it back to someone, someday soon.

Limit the effects of negative people.

Being out of work can feel like a good reason to get together with other people who see the world as darkly as you do at the moment. We've all done it at one time or another.

Grousing about one's problems with like-minded people can feel like belonging to a brotherhood or a sisterhood. But it's like acid that slowly wears away one of the most precious things you'll ever own: Your self-esteem.

So when something particularly unpleasant happens, take maybe half an hour to let it out. A heavy workout. A run in the park. Whatever you usually do to let off steam that's legal and productive.

Time it. If you think you need an hour, fine. Then after the hour, go back to your schedule. Work on that resume. Research that company. Whatever you had originally planned to do for that day.

Allowing yourself to feel bad for awhile tells you that you're human, you have the right to be upset and hurt and confused sometimes. Give yourself the time to deal with that. Then get back to work.

There are many negative people you can avoid but it's harder when they are family members. If it's your mother or your spouse, have a frank conversation with them. Tell them that what you need from them right now is their support. They play a vital role in helping you get back on your feet. Thank them in advance.

A word about job clubs. You could find one that is productive and supportive. Members are all searching for jobs and when they find some they can't apply for themselves, they share this information with the club. People get down at times but overall there is a feeling of excitement that they will soon be employed. That's the kind of club you want to join. If you find yourself in the other kind where most of the members gripe and not much progress is being made, feel free to Exit, Stage Left.

Embrace Change.

It's not easy to come from the days of typewriters and dial phones and computers that took up a whole room, to be dumped head-first into the twenty-first century. Text, Tweet, Twitter. Things are changing at an alarming rate.

It can be tough to get your mind around the speed of change, but when it comes to getting and keeping a job, you have to stay current with your industry.

One way to stay current is to cultivate friends of all ages, at work and in education and social settings. Younger friends can help enormously with understanding the latest technology. No, you won't be able to keep up with absolutely everything. But it sure helps when you know who to ask.

In return, you have a wealth of experience for them to draw on.

Get used to working with (much) younger people.

Does it bother you to have to work with younger people, maybe even a much younger supervisor?

I am lucky because I had to learn to work with people much younger than me on important projects. Years ago my husband and I returned to university. We were thirty-somethings in classes with eighteen-year-olds. There was lots of group work and we were surprised to know that those eighteen-year-olds could teach us a lot. (By the way, we got a ten-year-old kid to help us with the computer graphics assignments.)

More recently I was in a workplace where most of the people were at least twenty years younger than me. They had a different approach to work, a much more casual one. Being the good Boomer that I was, I'd come in and sit down at my desk about fifteen minutes before work started, as though marching to the tick tock of an invisible time clock.

The others would come in and sit down as though they had just sauntered in from watching TV in the living room. And their dress was casual — it seemed like anything was okay.

They also took a number of unofficial breaks during the day, where I would check my watch for the appropriate break time, and, again, minding that invisible time clock, would be back at my desk promptly at 10:30.

But guess what? For all their informal attitude to work, the work got done. And they were very good at it, especially the computer work. They were also open and helpful whenever I had a problem (likely used to that from helping their parents).

And the workplace was fun, and fun is contagious. I remember one employee (a Boomer) sneaking up on a twenty-something and grabbing her clipboard. 'That's mine!' he said, and ran off down the hall with her in hot pursuit. The rest of us looked at each other, laughed, and yes, got back to work. My young supervisor said, 'Sometimes this is too much fun to be work'.

And what's wrong with that?

The Long Haul

17

How long will you be out of work?

Neither of us knows. You don't know when that phone call will come in for an interview or someone will call saying you got the job after last week's interview. It will likely be when you least expect it.

Until then you put one foot in front of the other. On the days that seem to last 48 hours, set yourself one small task and then another. Don't think too much.

Guard your energy like a miser.

Eat a healthy diet, exercise, get enough sleep.

Simple things, but things that will come back to bite you fairly quickly if you ignore them.

One of the biggest myths about older workers is that we don't have the energy of the twenty-somethings. That might be true, but we can maintain a good energy level by watching what we eat, being active at least once a day, and getting a full 7 to 8 hours of sleep each night.

Going to a community gym or walking with a group can also ease those feelings of loneliness. It might also provide some contacts which could lead you to a job opening. You never know who you will meet. The person working out beside you might have a spouse or best friend in your industry. Not that you're going to grill everyone you meet for a potential job, but by being friendly you can find out a lot of things.

Keeping healthy will also fight depression. It's not an option to stay positive while you're out of work. It's a necessity.

You need to laugh sometimes. One of the most precious things you own is your sense of humor. Guard it with your life.

Job hunting is a job in itself and a tough one. So put in your hours and effort and then give yourself a break. You need to mentally detach yourself from it or it will drive you mad.

And remember your passions. Find the time—even if it's just 15 minutes a day—to work on one of them.

"Because tomorrow the sun will rise. Who knows what the tide could bring in?"

- Tom Hanks as Chuck Noland in the movie Cast Away

Give this chapter to your spouse
(or other adult family members)

18

Okay, Spouse, let's get real here.

You've lost maybe a half or more of your household income with this layoff, firing, downsizing. You're scared, too. Maybe 'scared' doesn't begin to cover it. How about petrified?

This has happened to you, too, through no fault of your own. Part of you is screaming, "It's not fair! It's not fair!"

Go hit a pillow, run around the block, clean up the yard, or take every last box to recycling. Release that negative energy. And then come back to your spouse with a calm head and a good heart. That's what they need right now.

Now is the time that you have to be the stronger partner, at least for a while. You have to show your support even when (especially when) days are tough.

Your partner is facing not only the financial shock of losing a salary; he or she is worried that they might have had something to do with this. When you're let go from a job, no matter if it's a layoff and not your fault, there's always a little part of you that blames yourself for what happened and most of all, for putting your family in this position. That's what your partner is likely feeling right now.

In the case of a layoff there was probably nothing they could have done to keep their job. And even if they could have done something, now is not the time for recriminations. Now is the time for support.

There's a lot of fear that goes along with losing a job. They need a hug, unconditional understanding, and later, the comfort of having a non-judgmental partner help them with a plan. That's what you would want, too.

So for the moment put aside your fears of how you'll pay the rent or the mortgage. Take a deep breath. In a long relationship, there will be huge ups and downs. You've probably got through worse in your lives. You will survive this one, too.

That doesn't mean you have to sit by while your partner slowly slips into a depression. If you find they aren't listening to you, think of a buddy they respect and try to get your partner to talk to him or her.

Choose the best time to talk about the nitty gritty when both of you are fairly calm. Start with the worst case scenario. Worst case as in, my spouse won't be able to find a job for a year.

Should we move? Sell the house and rent? Move in with family for a short time? What about temporary jobs? How far are we willing to drive each day for a job? How about moving for a job in another city?

It's good to acknowledge the elephant in the room. Much harder to move around him without admitting he's there.

Once you've looked at the worst you'll begin to relax. The worst is not likely to happen. If you have relatives who have lived through the Depression, you know your present situation isn't that bad.

Sometimes it's just a matter of not saying anything when your impulse is to make a hurtful comment. That comment might make you feel better for a few moments but the look in your partner's eyes will haunt you and make you feel much worse.

It's important to have times when no one is thinking about the bills. Go for a walk in the park. Pick flowers with the grandkids. Go for a swim. Do something fun (and free) that won't remind you of the present worrying circumstances, if only for a couple of hours. That's an order.

Losing a job sucks. But there is a reason for all things. In a year or two you might find that you were stronger than you ever imagined. If you can get through this, then the smaller annoyances of life are just that—annoyances. You've been through boot camp here.

Maybe this layoff gave your spouse more time to reconnect with the kids, or the chance to change an occupation that obviously wasn't going anywhere. Or maybe you found you had to live on much less so that when another job came into your lives, you were able to save money for the mortgage, the kids' schooling, or a vacation.

This is your time to shine, to show your character. It's in you.

Crystal Ball

19

After reading this book you will still be over 50 but hopefully on your way to new employment.

And then what?

There's been a lot of talk about what will happen when the Baby Boomers retire. A few years ago, someone predicted that we would leave the workforce en masse and send the pension system into a nosedive as we stood in line for our benefits. Not to mention the havoc that would follow when we started using all those assets, many inherited from our Depression-era parents.

But the Boomers were never predictable. The big labor shortage that was supposed to follow the wave of Boomer retirement likely won't be as drastic as predicted. So if you're a younger Boomer hoping to grab those jobs recently vacated by your older siblings, it might not happen. Some of us will retire at 65, but likely many more of us won't.

The best guess is that some will retire in luxury, some will still work part time or full time because we have to or we want to. And some of us will be so valuable that we will be called out of retirement more than once.

Constant leisure would be my idea of hell. I won't be golfing in Florida but I don't want to be scraping a car of ice and snow at 6 a.m. when I'm 65.

I'll always be writing, God willing. It's the kind of occupation that you can't just shut off when you're 65. And for the all the frustrations, it's still so much fun.

Forget the statistics. You have to draw your own picture of retirement and step into it.

So to those of us who aren't 20 anymore—

Good luck and have a happy life.

> *When one door of happiness closes, another opens; but often we look so long at the closed door that we do not see the one which has been opened for us.*
>
> \- *Helen Keller*